Colorful Swearing Dreams

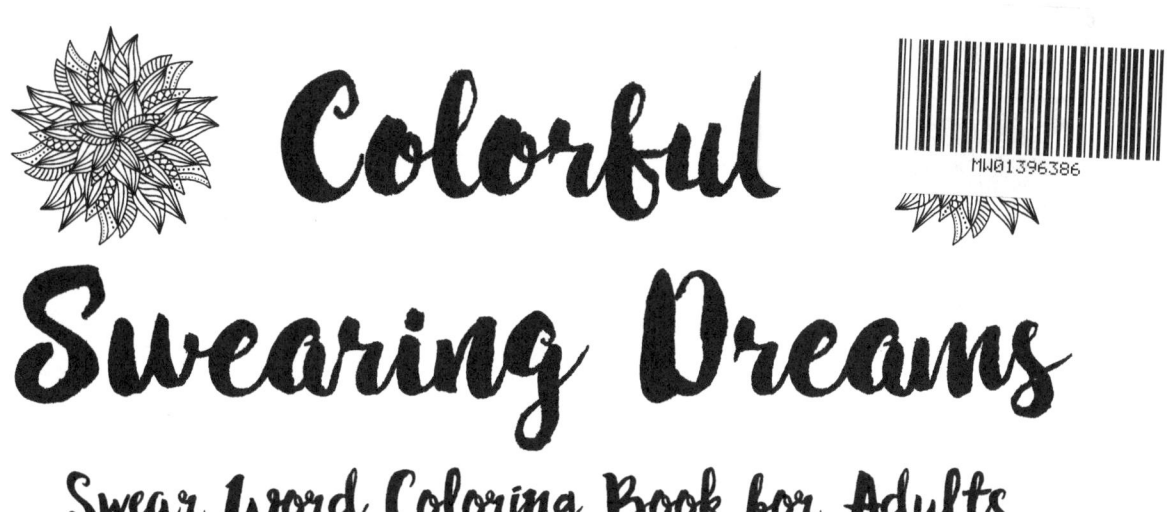

Swear Word Coloring Book for Adults

IS YOUR STRESS LEVEL HIGH?
DO YOU WANT TO SWEAR OUT LOUD
TO LEVEL IT DOWN?
THIS BOOK WILL KICK YOUR STRESS AWAY!

Multiple studies revealed that coloring mandalas, geometric patterns & other shapes helps reduce stress and anxiety for adults.

This swear word coloring book will allow you to enter in a relaxed state by focusing in what you are doing and blocking out the nonstop thinking or other distractions. Those swear word designs will make you laugh and relieve your stress by expelling your negative thoughts.

This book contains 20 pages of beautiful & intricate designs mixing up with funny swear words that will connect with you.
Each page is single-sided for getting the best coloring experience.

TIME TO COLOR THE STRESS AWAY!

All Rights Reserved. Colorful Swearing Dreams

No part of this book may be reproduced, stored in a retrieval system, or transmitted in any form or by any means, electronic, mechanical, photocopying, recording, or otherwise, without the prior written permission of the author.

Colorful Swearing Dreams

Swear Word Coloring Book for Adults

Coloring Test Page

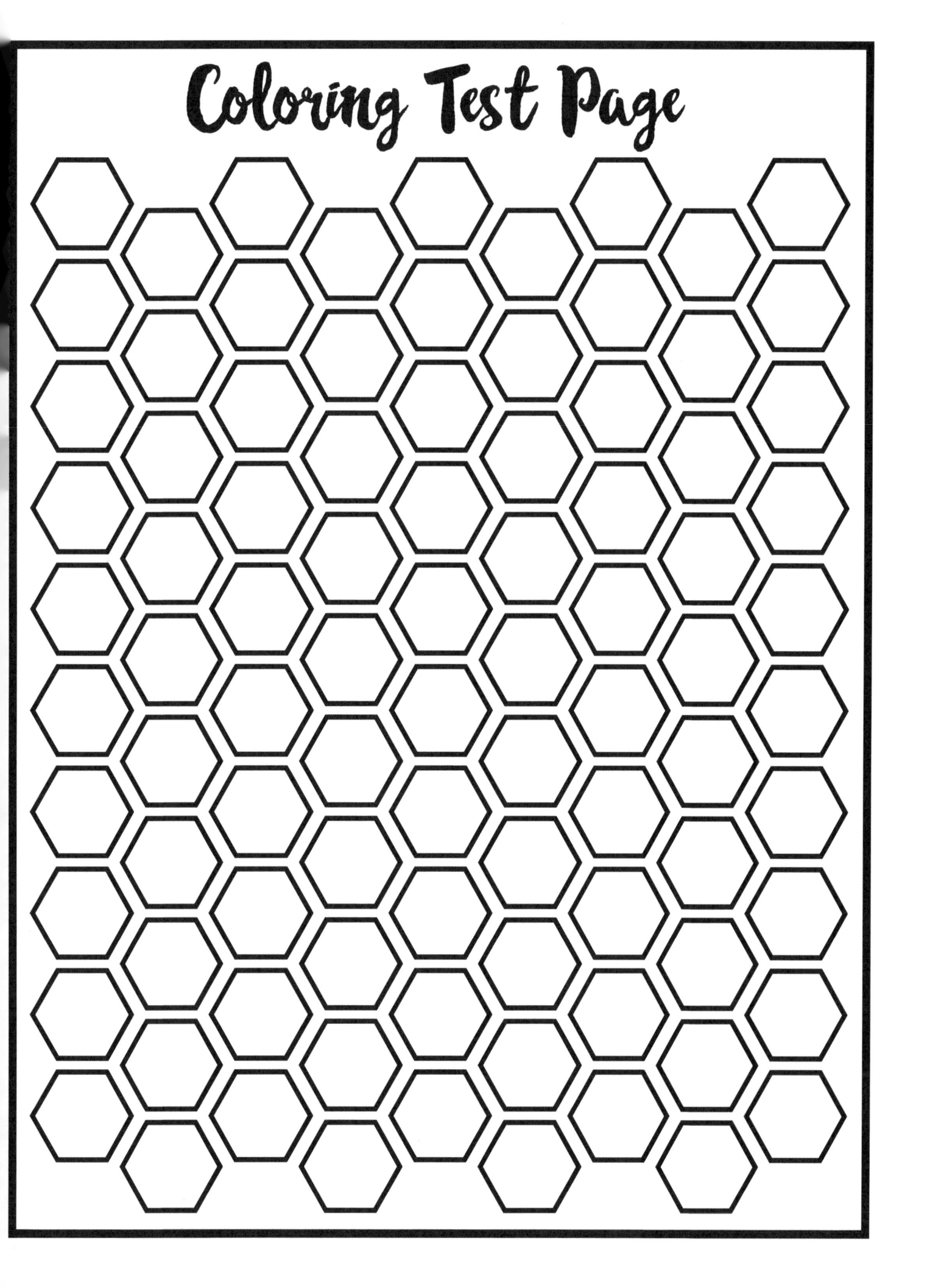

Colorful Swearing Dreams

Swear Word Coloring Book for Adults

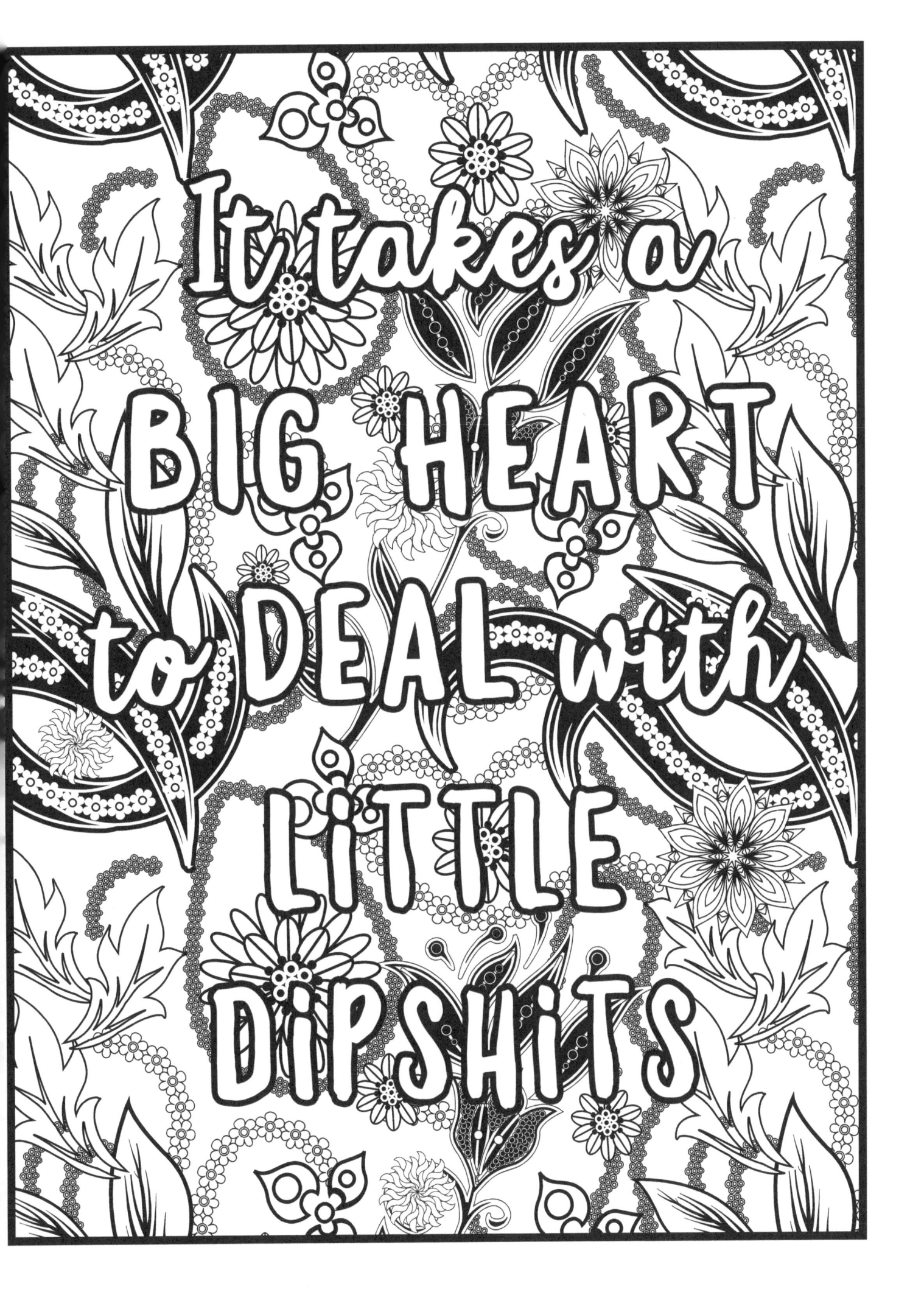

It takes a BIG HEART to DEAL with LITTLE DIPSHITS

Colorful Swearing Dreams

Swear Word Coloring Book for Adults

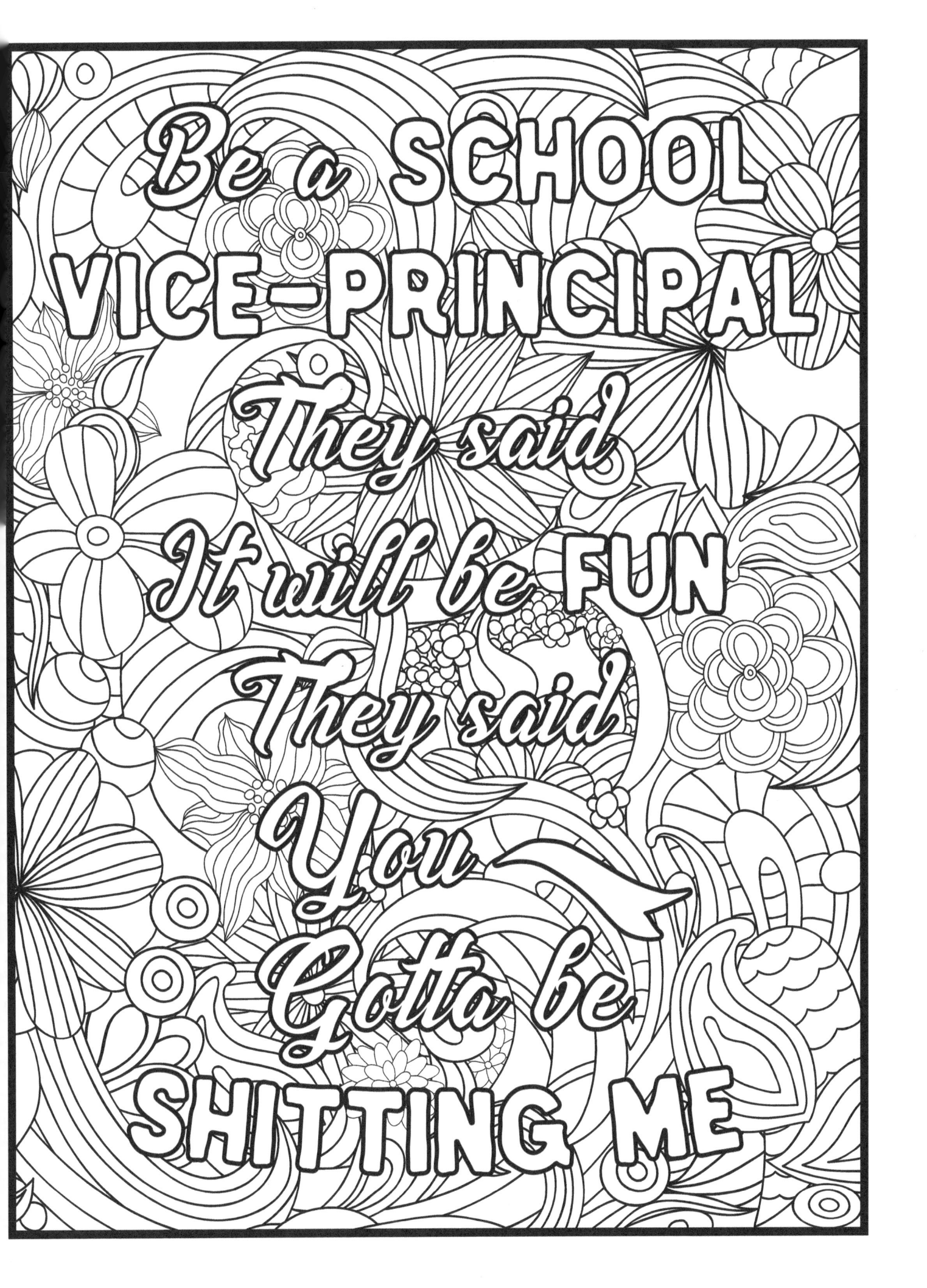

Be a SCHOOL VICE-PRINCIPAL They said It will be FUN They said You Gotta be SHITTING ME

Colorful Swearing Dreams

Swear Word Coloring Book for Adults

I've tried to STOP SWEARING But I CUNT

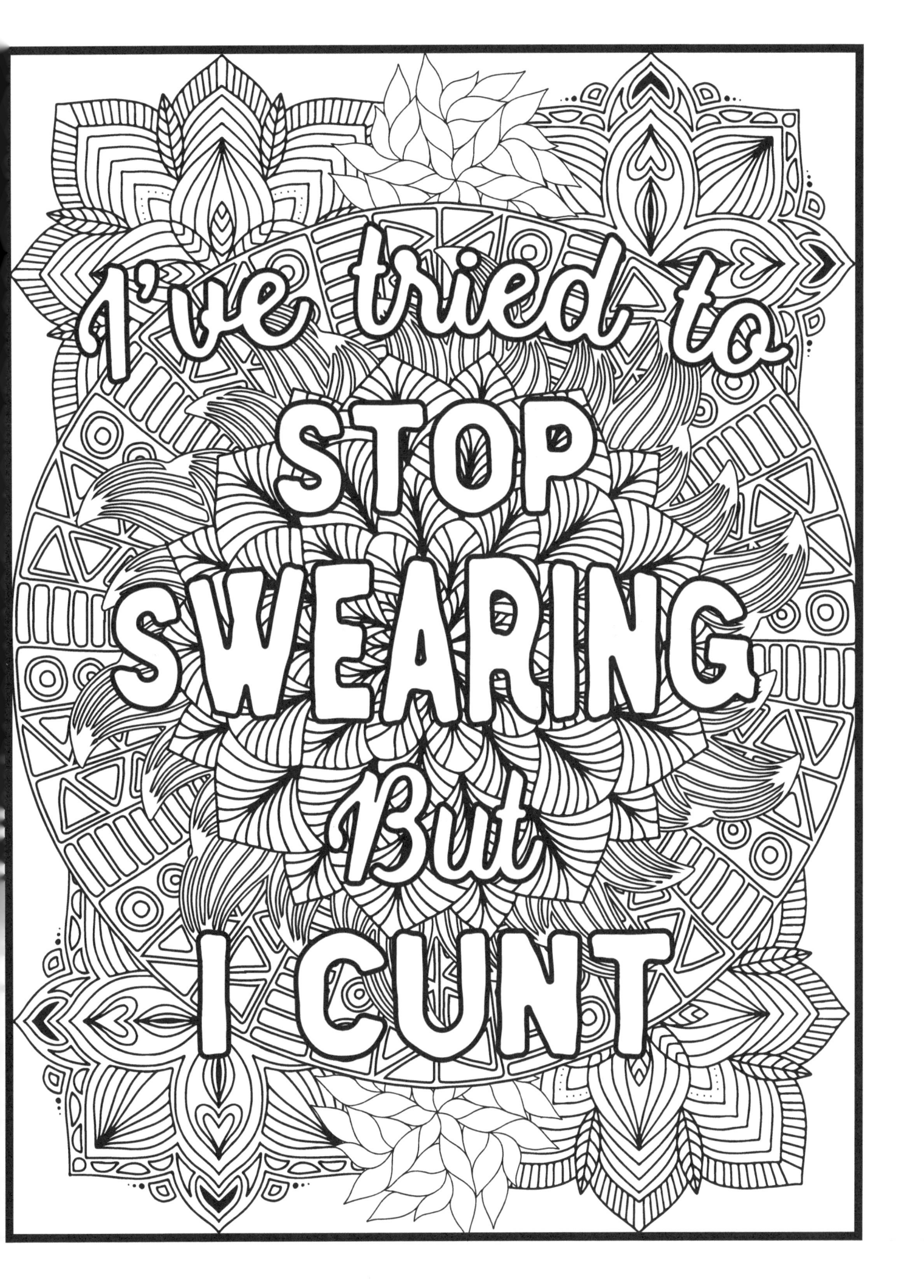

Colorful Swearing Dreams
Swear Word Coloring Book for Adults

I'm a VICE PRINCIPAL I'm not a FUCKING MAGICIAN

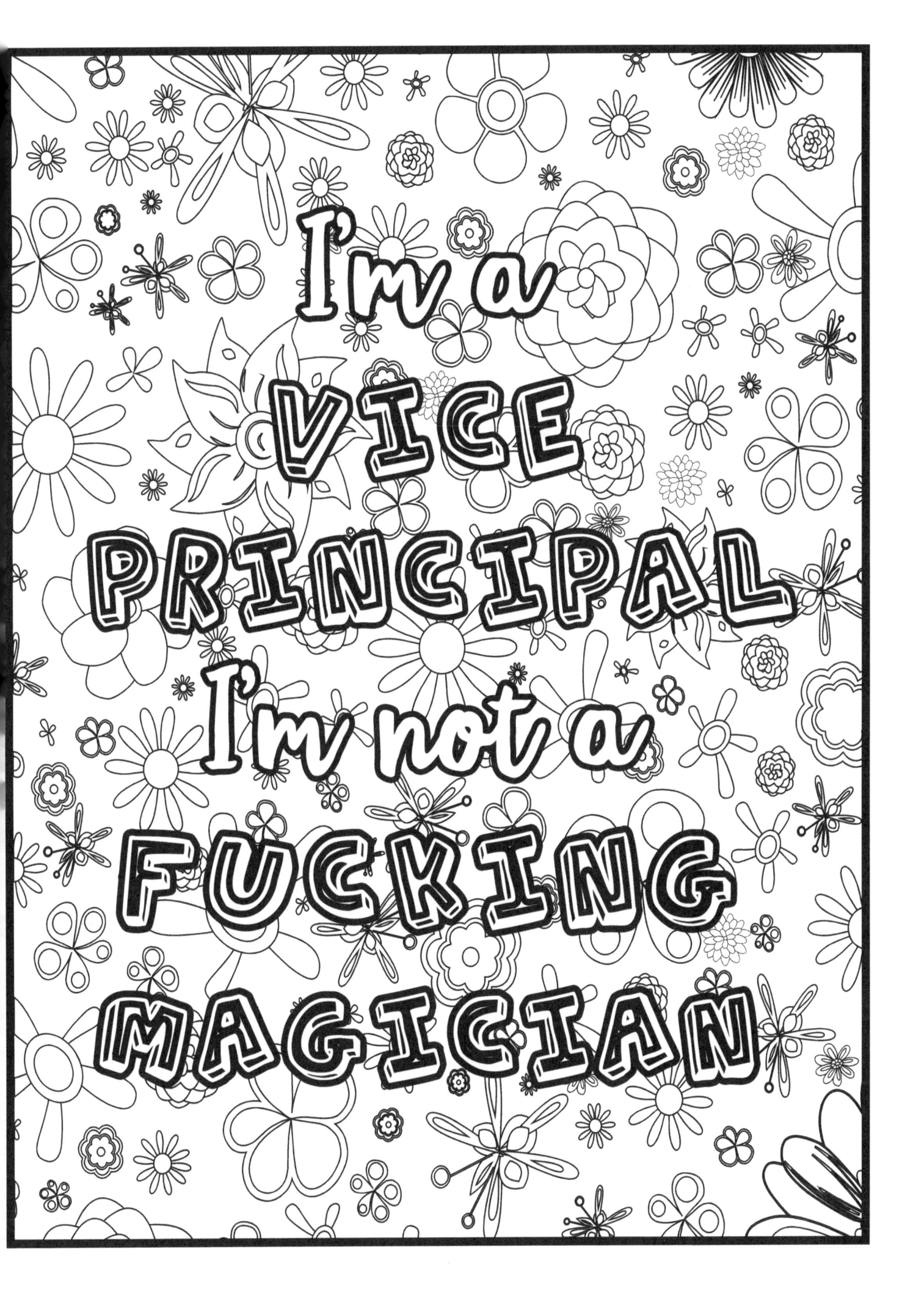

Colorful Swearing Dreams

Swear Word Coloring Book for Adults

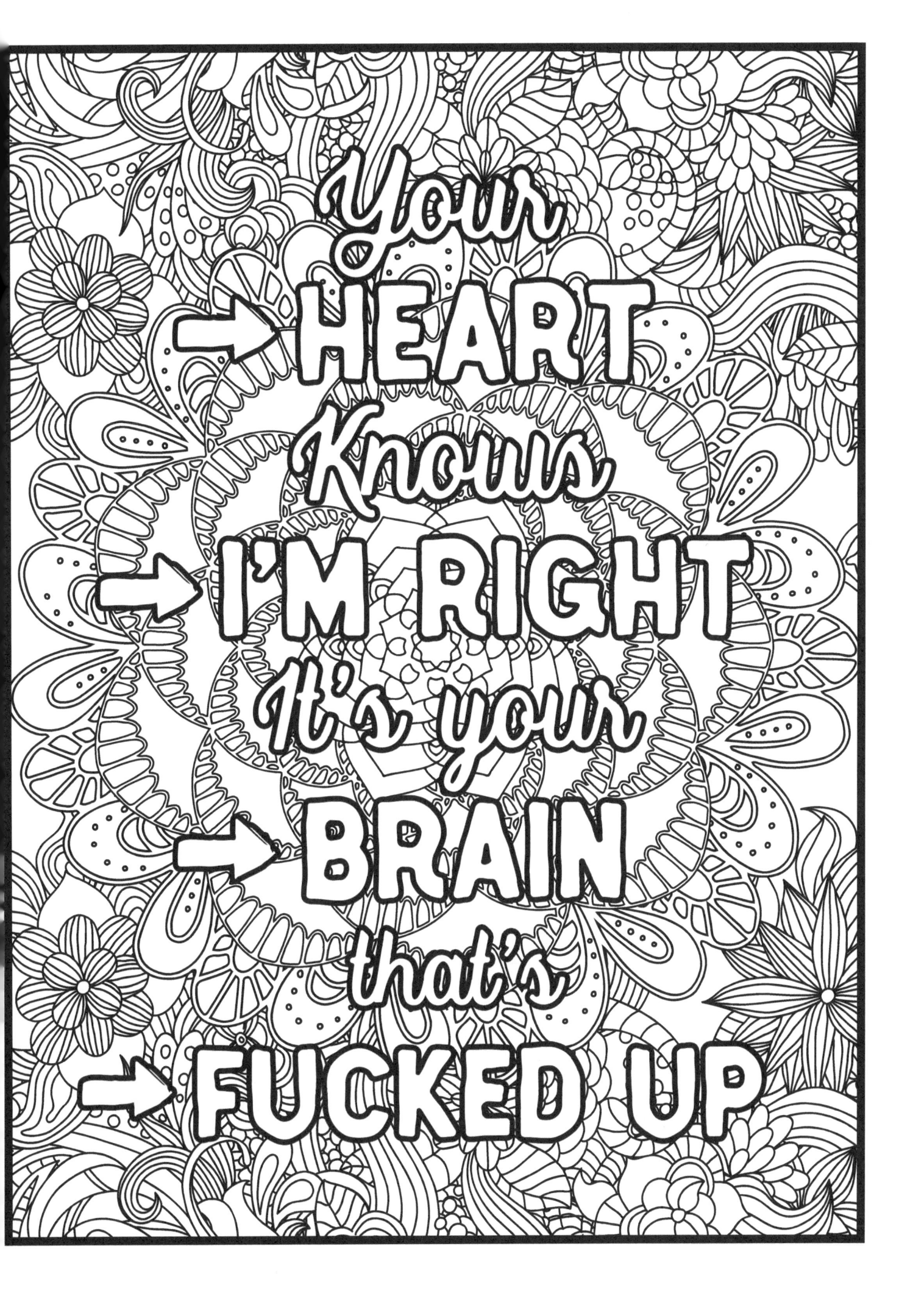

Your HEART knows I'M RIGHT It's your BRAIN that's FUCKED UP

Colorful Swearing Dreams

Swear Word Coloring Book for Adults

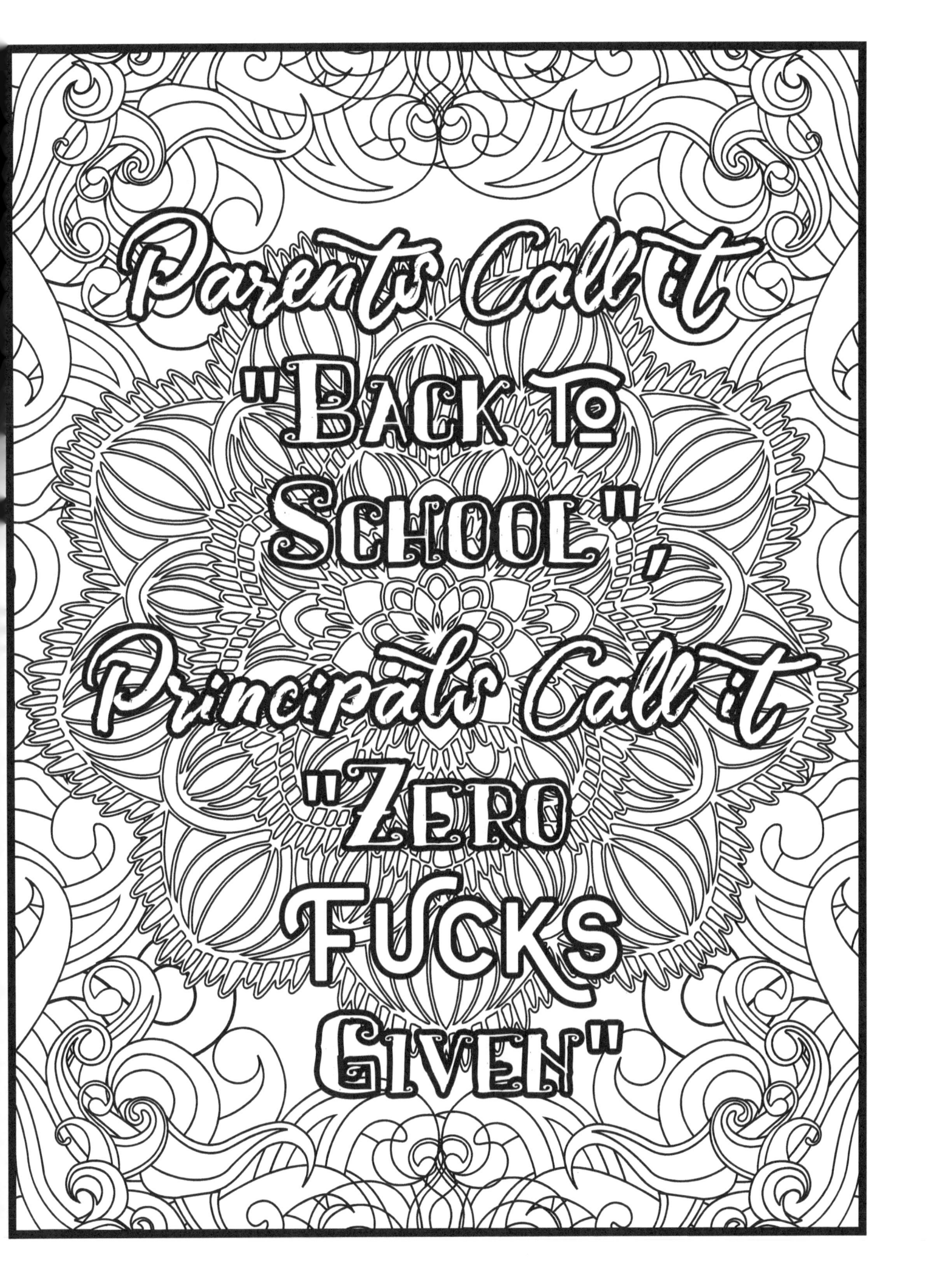

Parents Call it "Back To School", Principals Call it "Zero Fucks Given"

Colorful Swearing Dreams

Swear Word Coloring Book for Adults

Bullies: You Better Pray Mother Fuckers

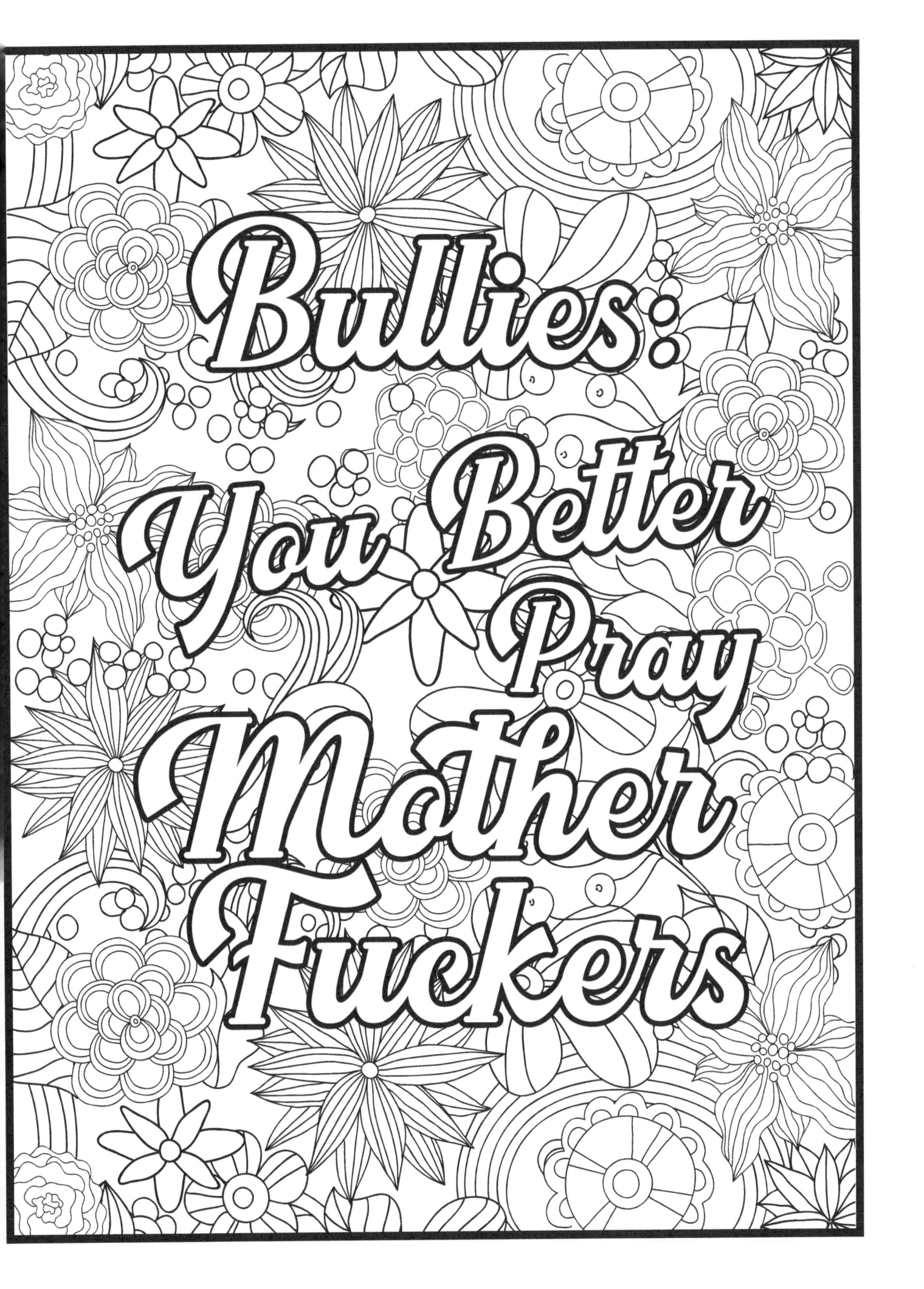

Colorful Swearing Dreams

Swear Word Coloring Book for Adults

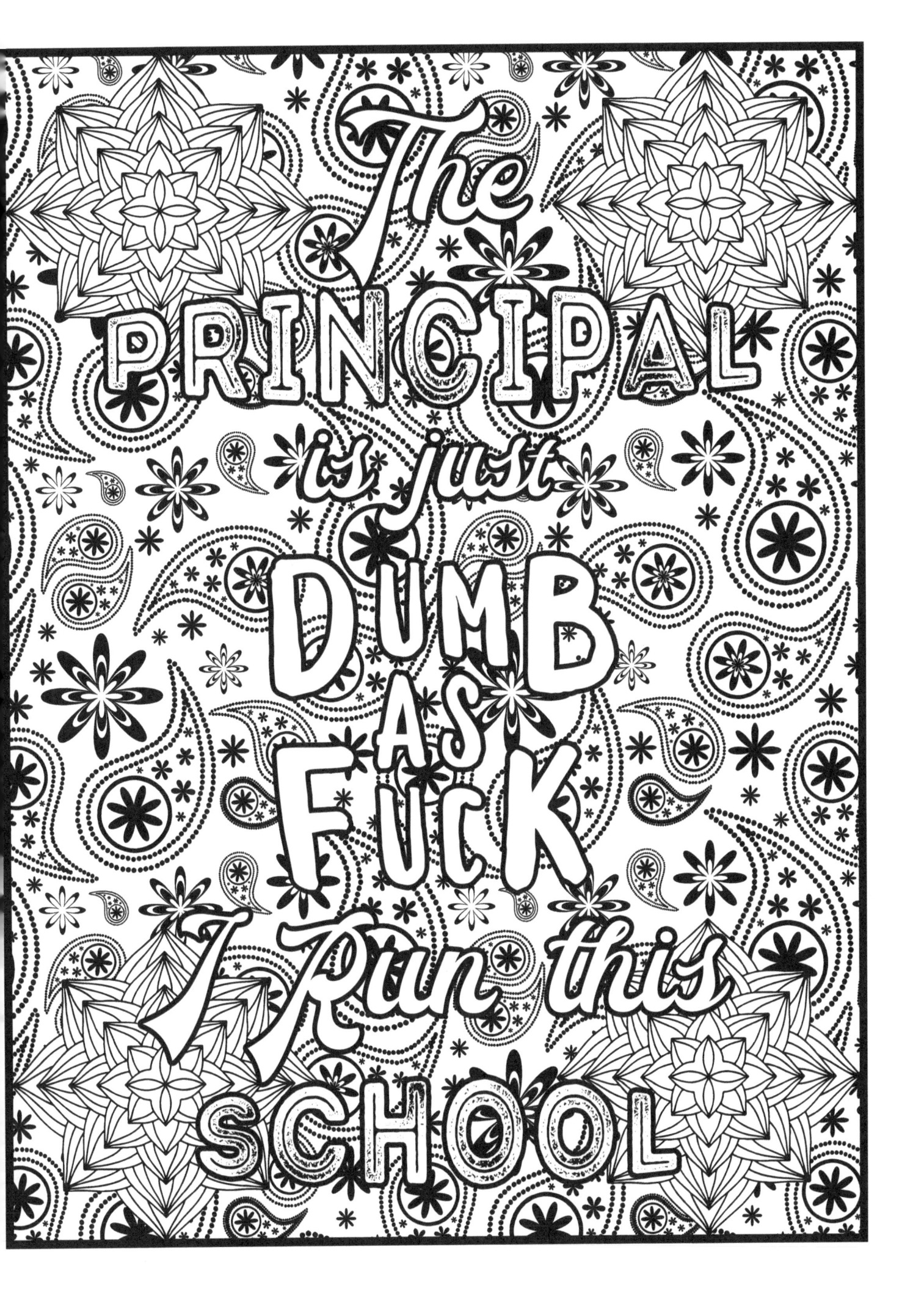

The Principal is just Dumb as Fuck I Run this School

Colorful Swearing Dreams

Swear Word Coloring Book for Adults

GET YOUR GODDAMN ASS in the PRINCIPAL'S OFFICE

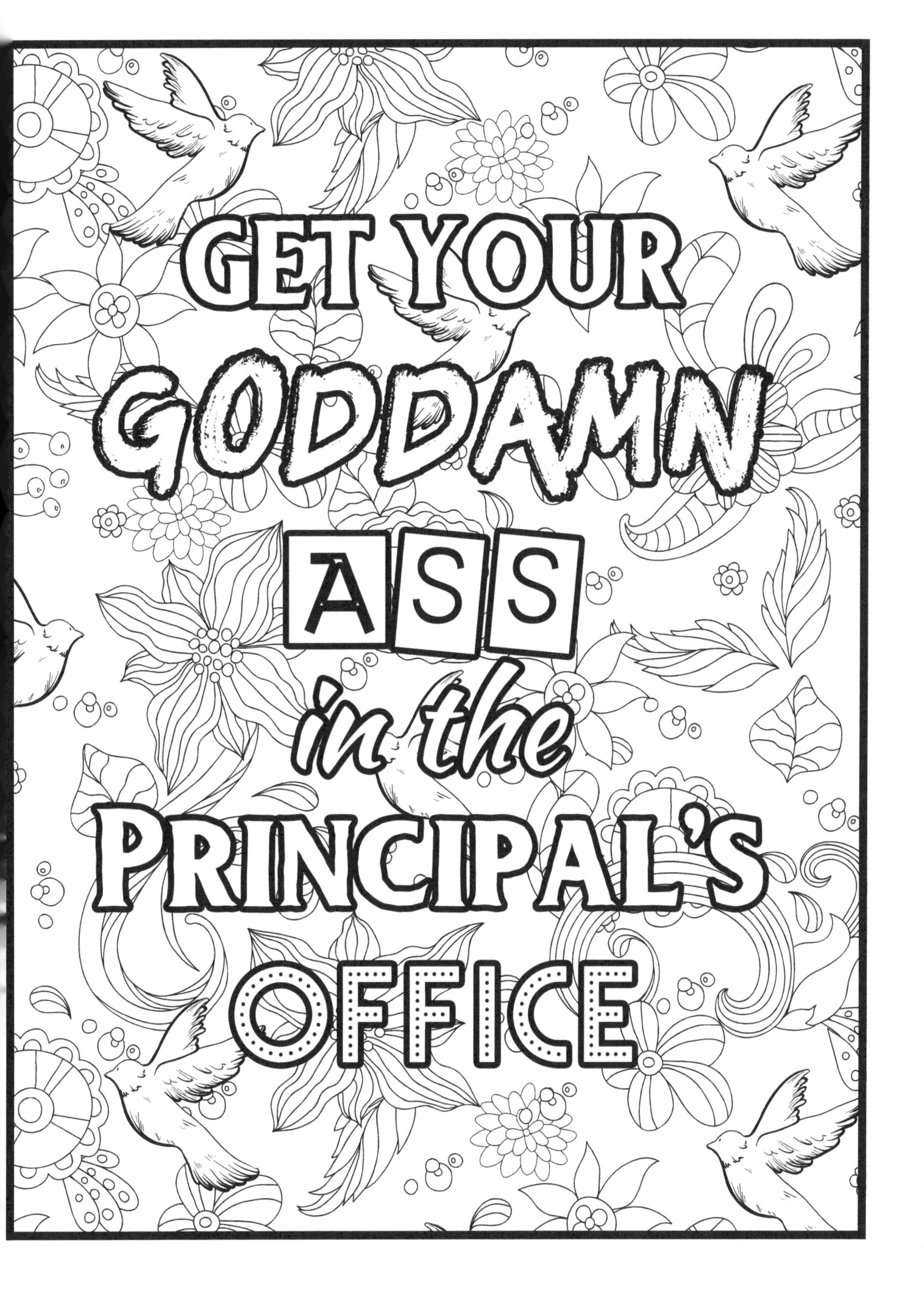

Colorful Swearing Dreams

Swear Word Coloring Book for Adults

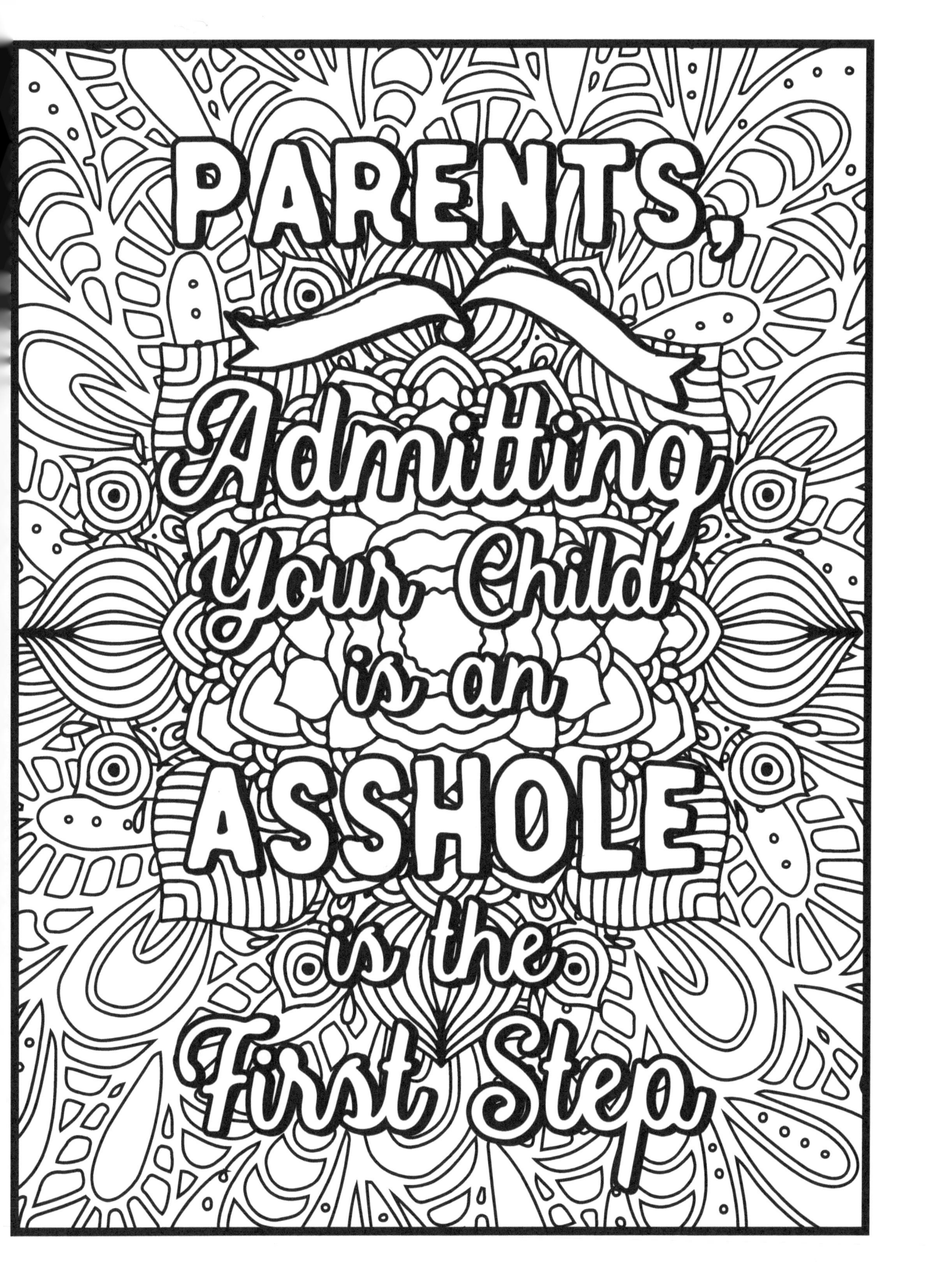

PARENTS, Admitting Your Child is an ASSHOLE is the First Step

Colorful Swearing Dreams

Swear Word Coloring Book for Adults

FUCK OFF MONDAY

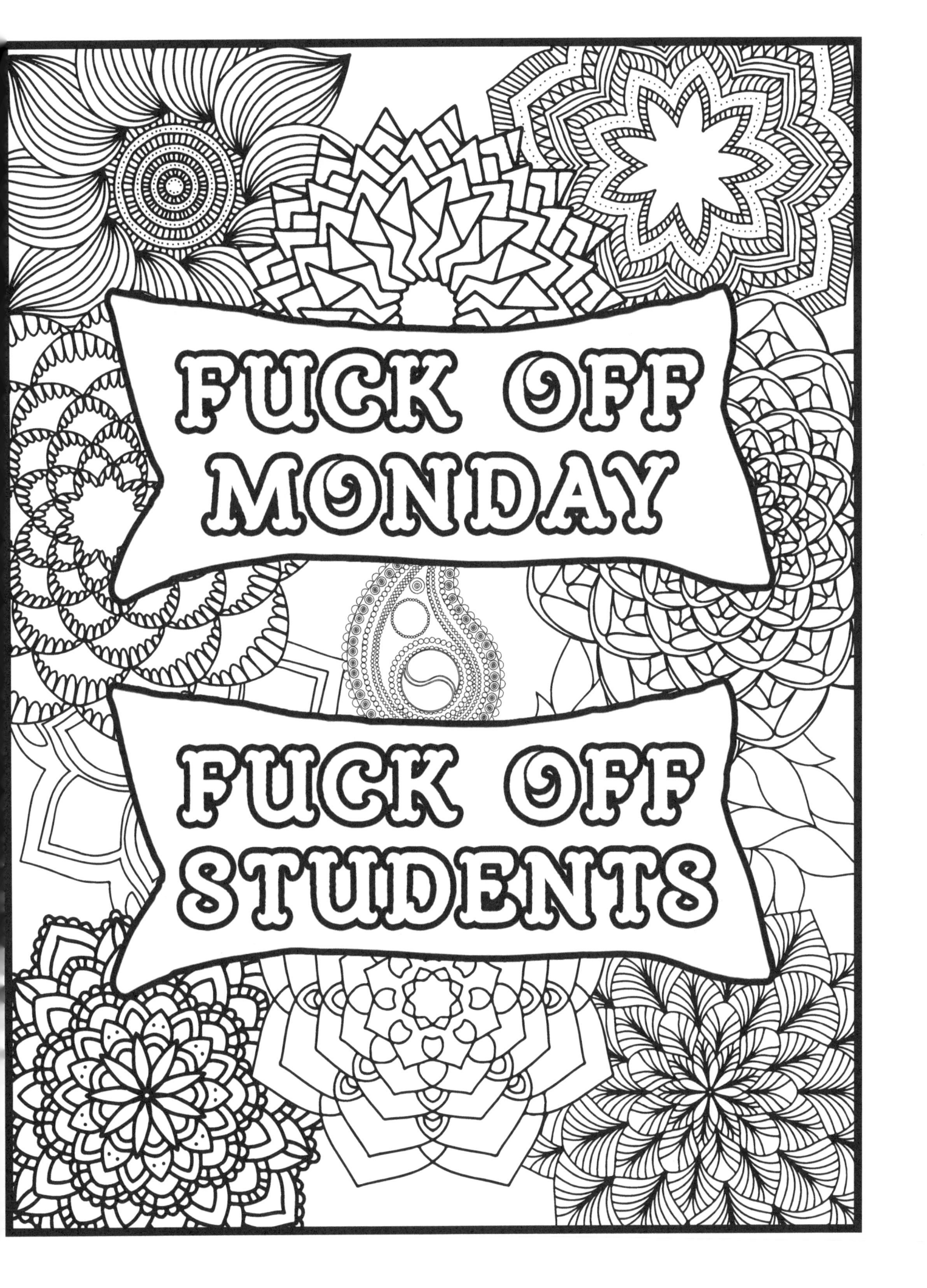

FUCK OFF STUDENTS

Colorful Swearing Dreams

Swear Word Coloring Book for Adults

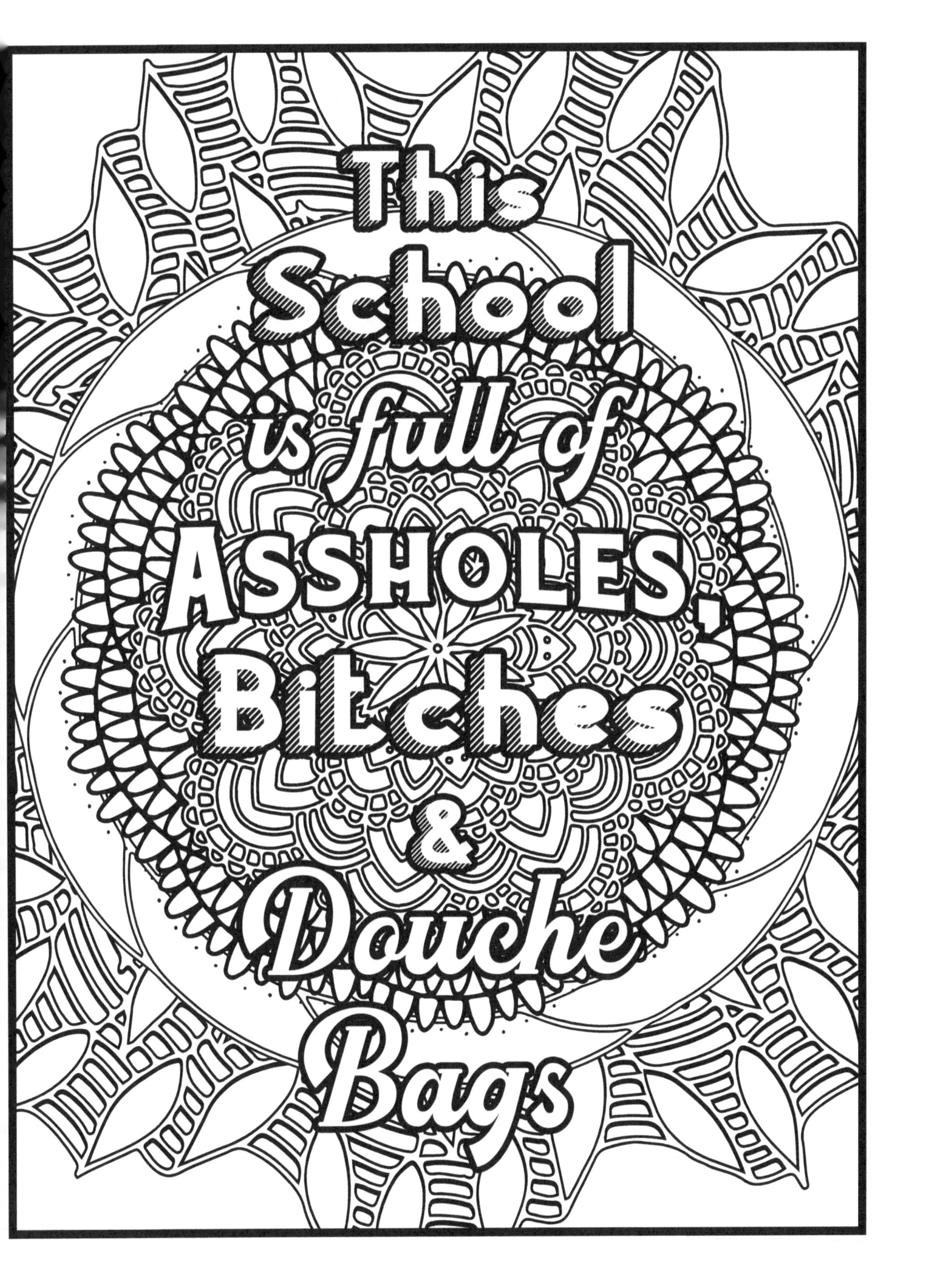

This School is full of ASSHOLES, Bitches & Douche Bags

Colorful Swearing Dreams

Swear Word Coloring Book for Adults

MANAGING *Fucktards* is HARD

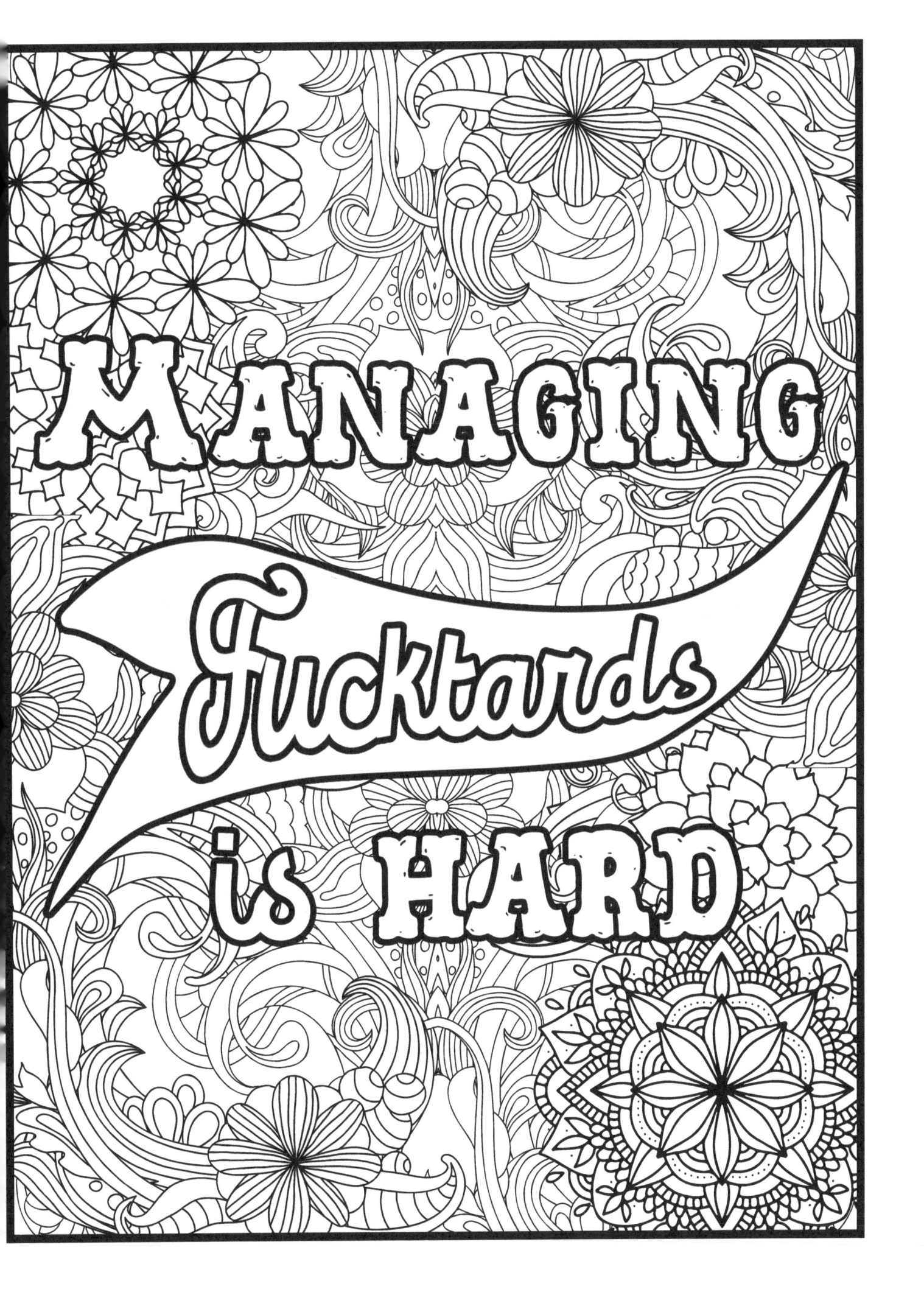

Colorful Swearing Dreams

Swear Word Coloring Book for Adults

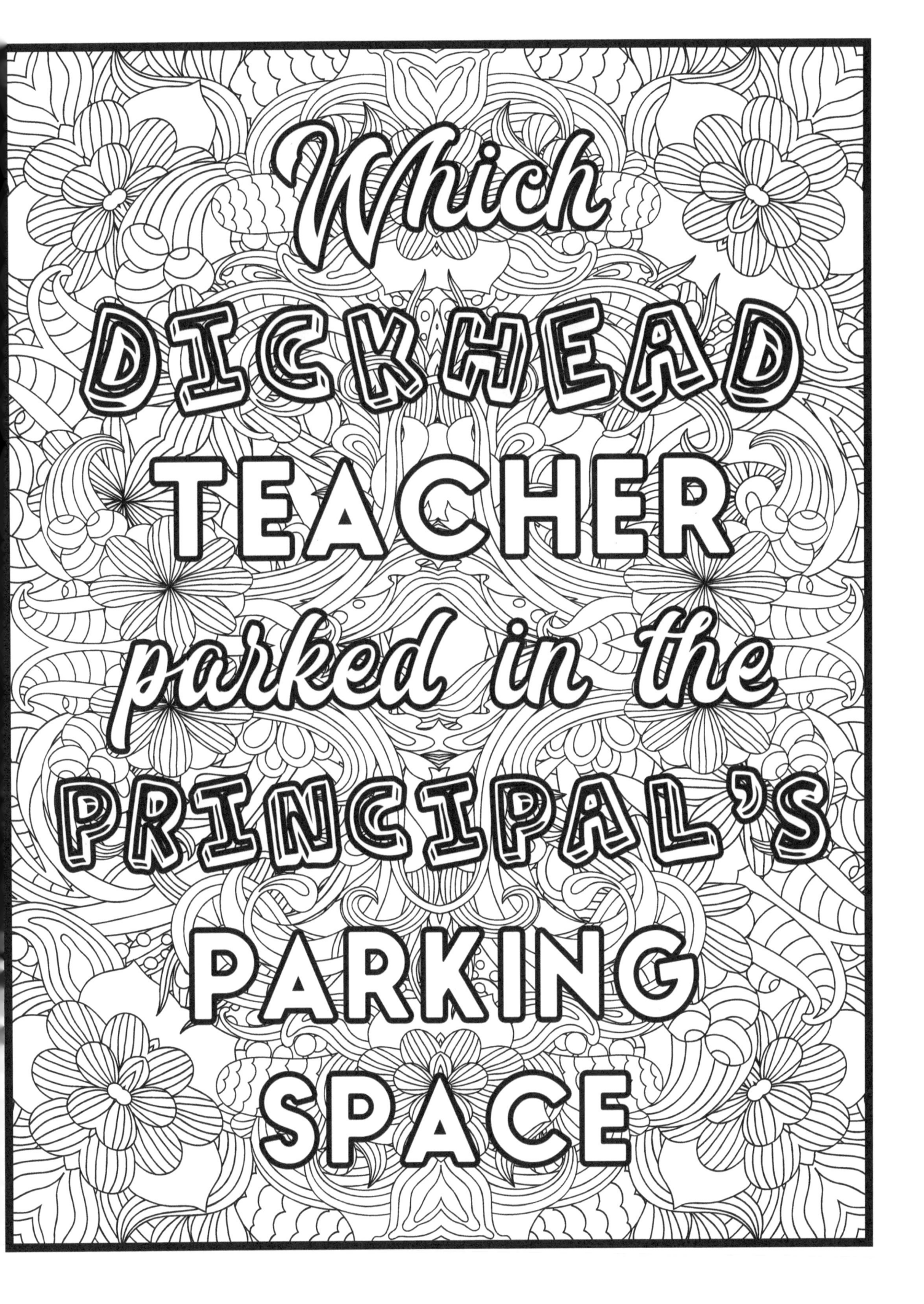

Which DICKHEAD TEACHER parked in the PRINCIPAL'S PARKING SPACE

Colorful Swearing Dreams

Swear Word Coloring Book for Adults

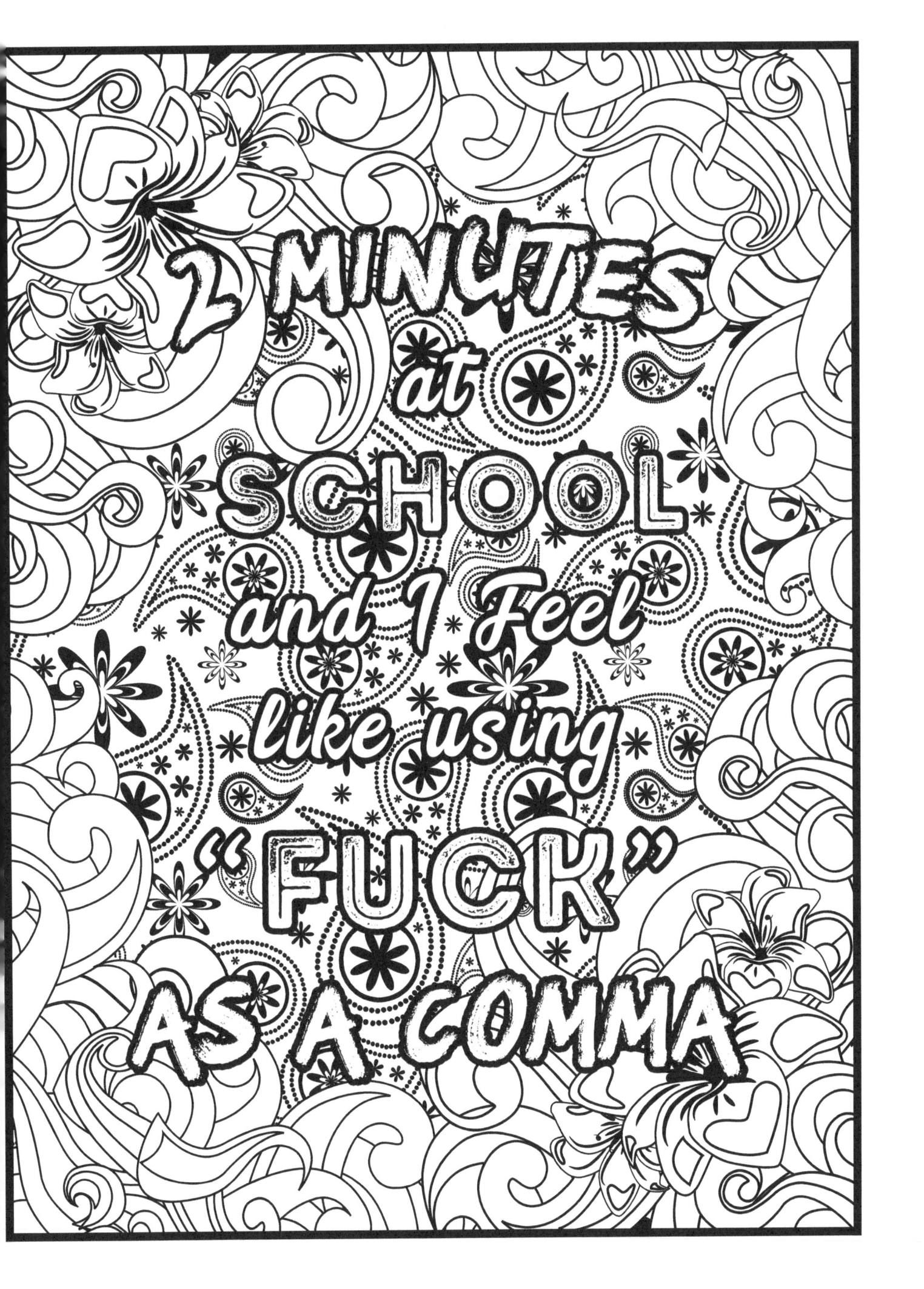

2 MINUTES at SCHOOL and I feel like using "FUCK" AS A COMMA

Colorful Swearing Dreams

Swear Word Coloring Book for Adults

I'm FRESH Out of FUCKS to Give Today

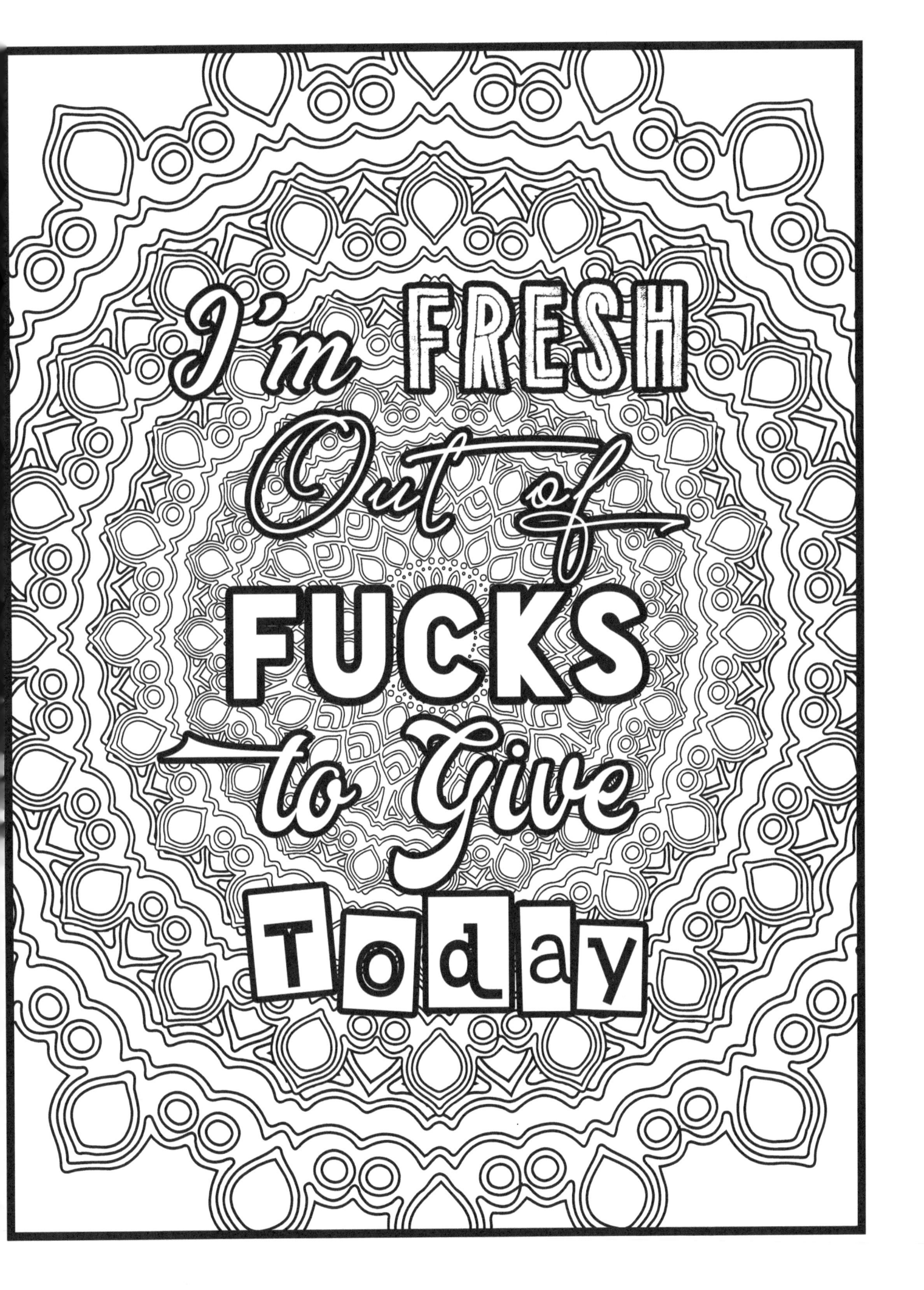

Colorful Swearing Dreams

Swear Word Coloring Book for Adults

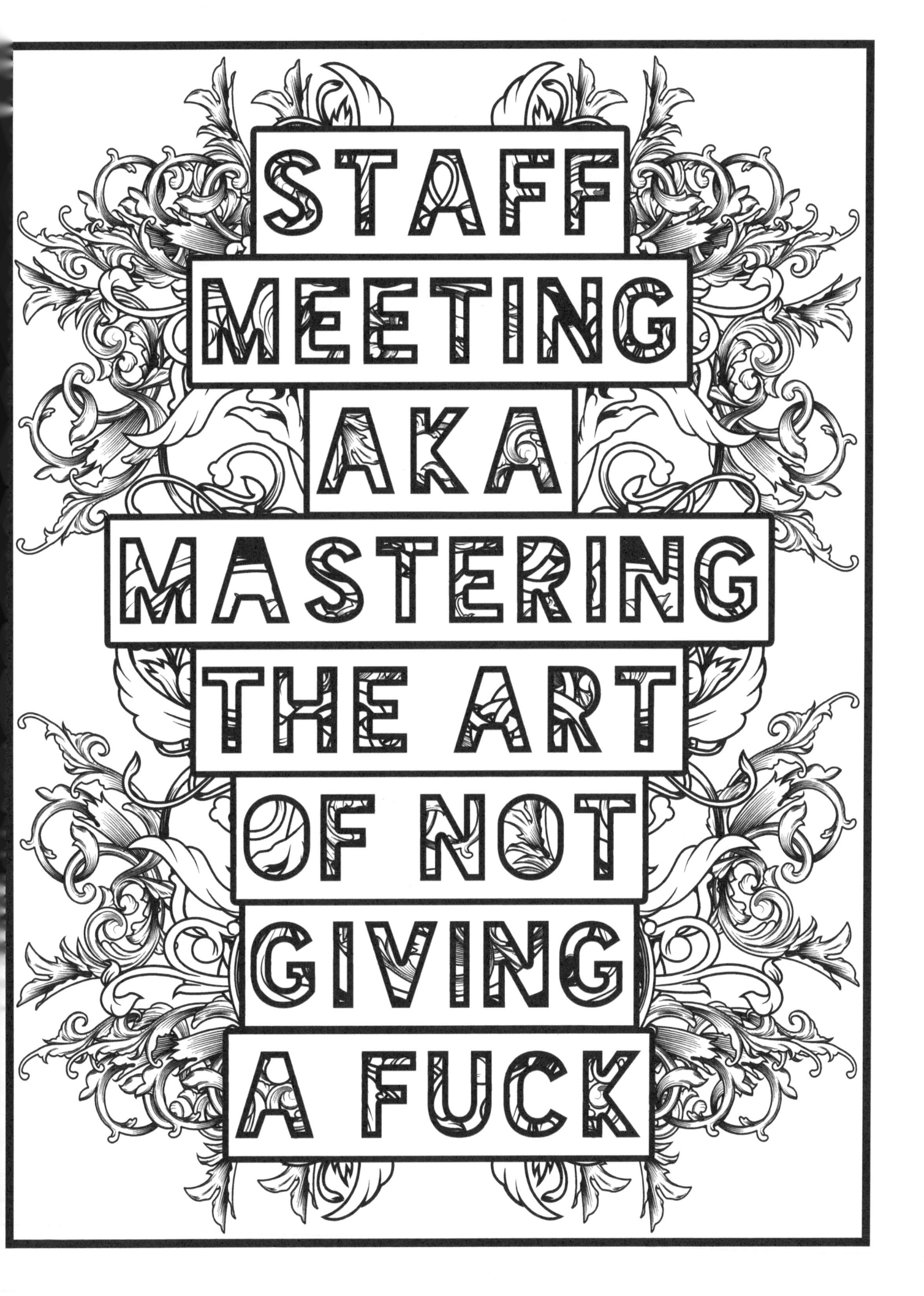

STAFF MEETING AKA MASTERING THE ART OF NOT GIVING A FUCK

Colorful Swearing Dreams
Swear Word Coloring Book for Adults

WHITEBOARDS are WHITE STUDENTS are ASSHOLES

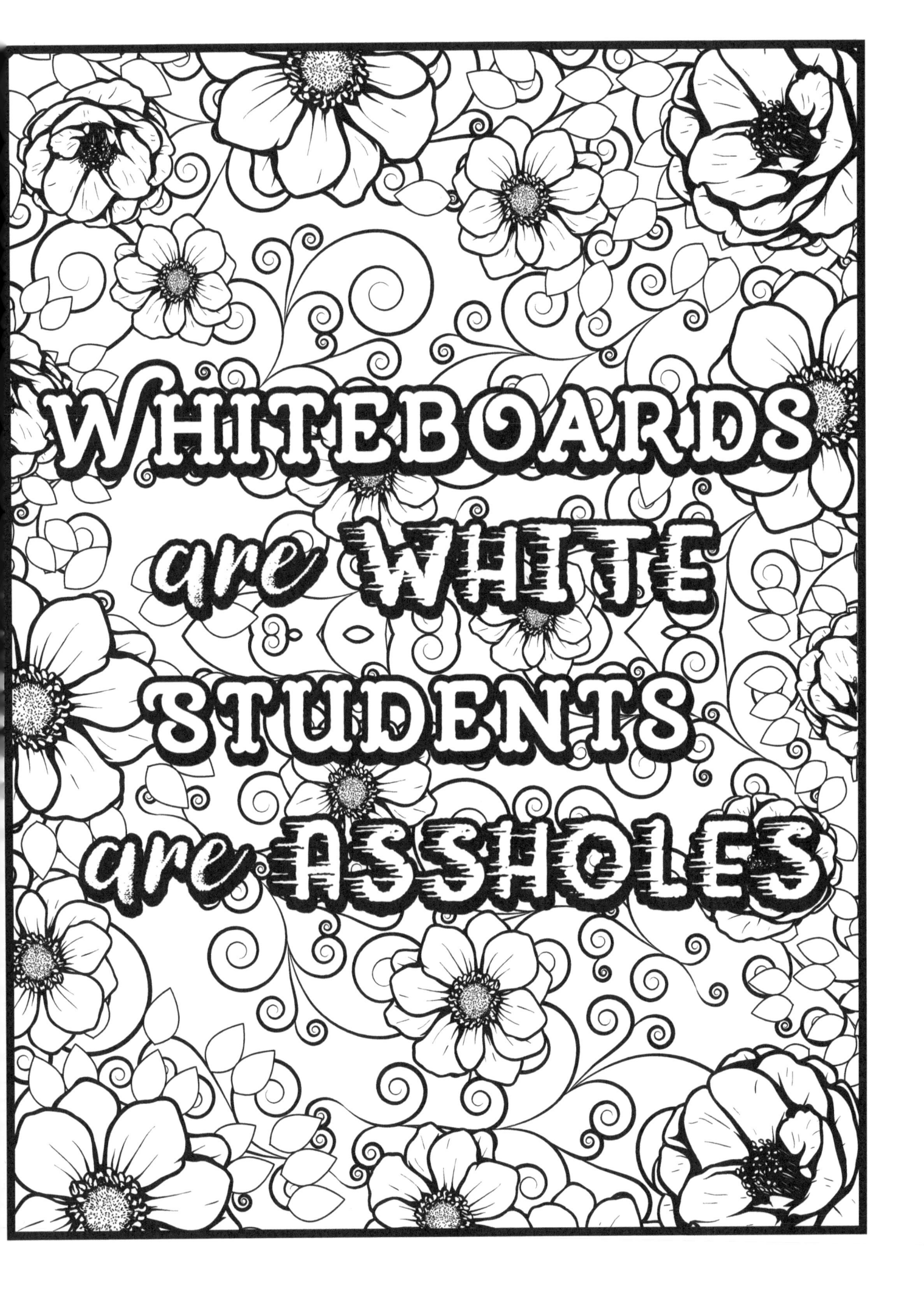

Colorful Swearing Dreams

Swear Word Coloring Book for Adults

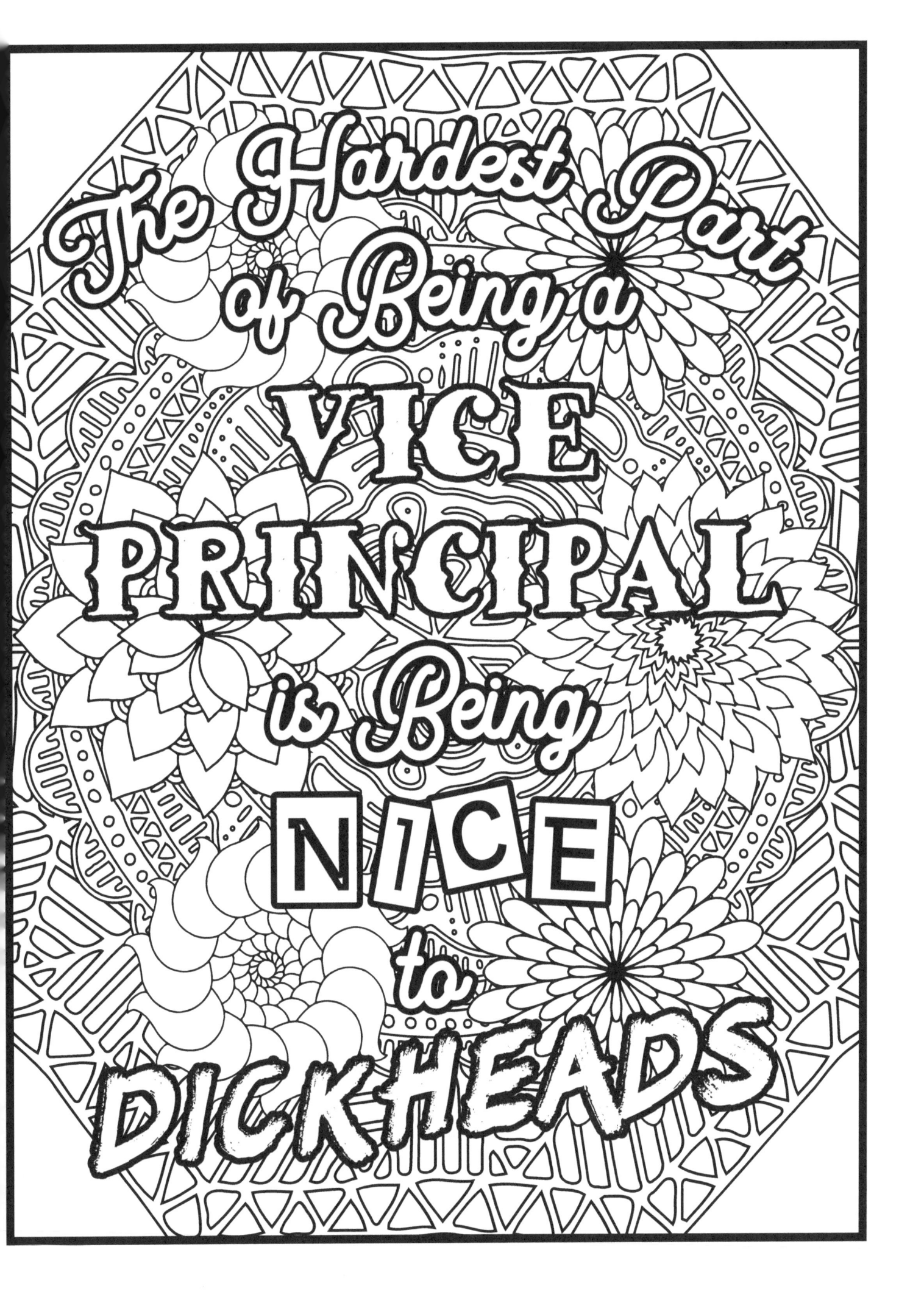

The Hardest Part of Being a VICE PRINCIPAL is Being NICE to DICKHEADS

Colorful Swearing Dreams

Swear Word Coloring Book for Adults

I hear FIFTY SHADES of BULLSHIT Everyday

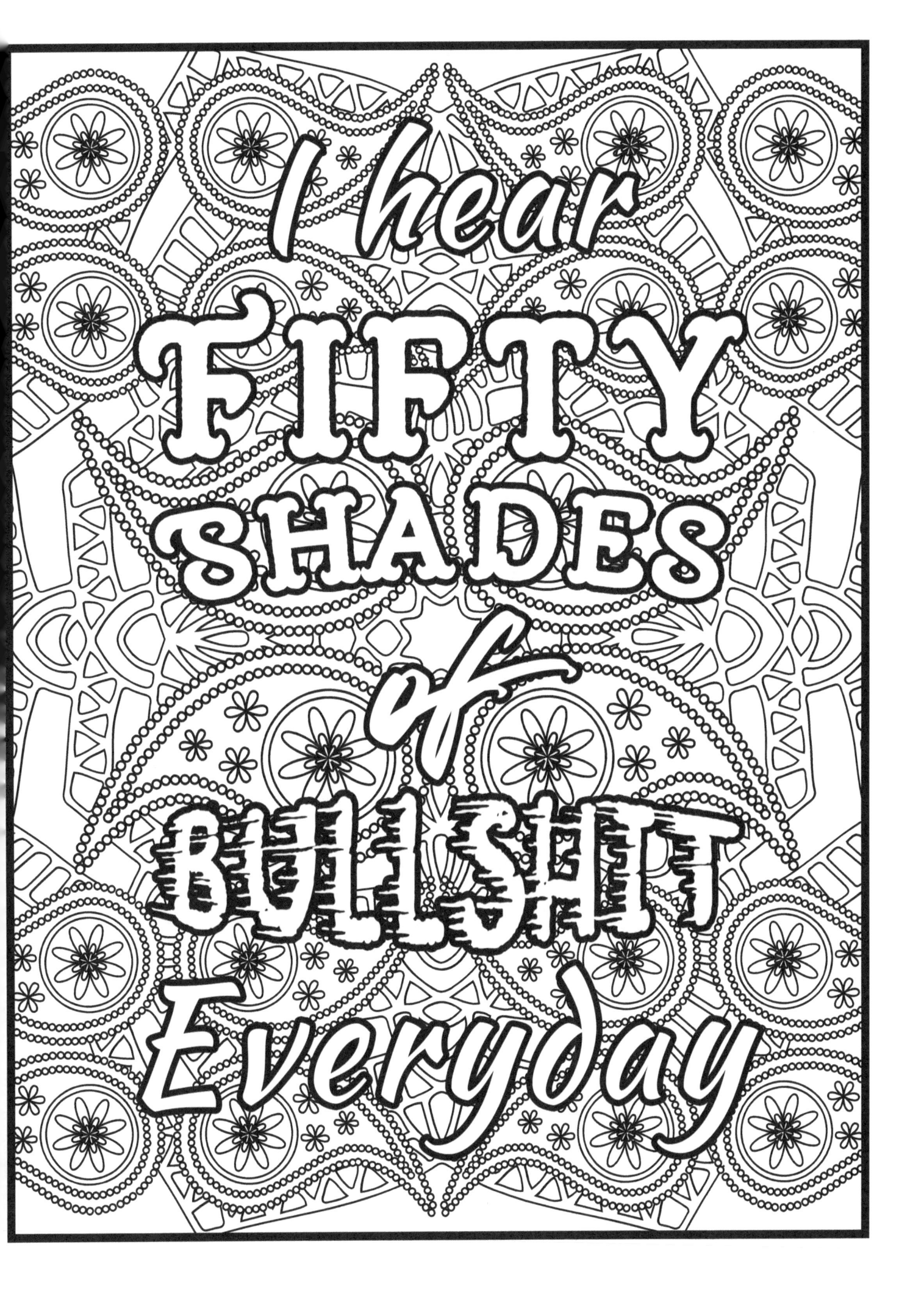

Colorful Swearing Dreams

Swear Word Coloring Book for Adults

Colorful Swearing Dreams

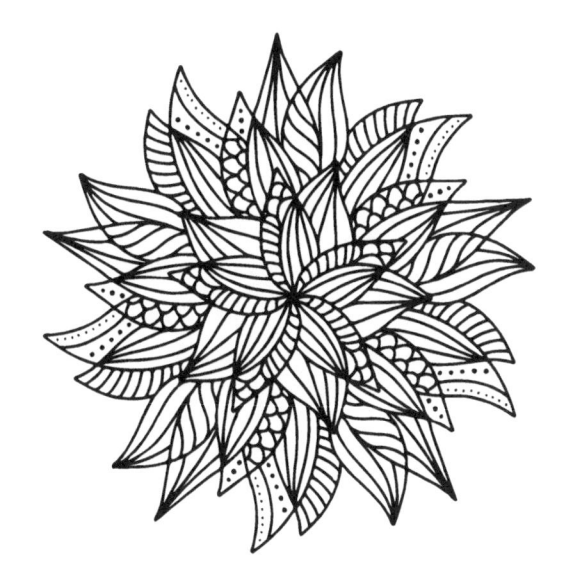

How is your stress level now?

Would you be kind enough to review our book?

Did the book allow you to put all the stress out of your mind, body and soul?
Hopefully you now feel fulfilled, relaxed and happy.

We sure put a lot of effort to provide you the best product possible that fits all your needs.

YOUR REVIEW is extremely valuable to us.
We don't see it as just a star rating, we read and study the feedbacks so we can consistently improve our products to shape them how you want them to be.

We take pride in making quality products for your satisfaction.

That is why, we would really appreciate if you can take few minutes of your time and leave us a review on our product's page.
That way, not only you will help other customers to make the right decision but you will also allow us to make other quality products that can make funny & unique gifts for your friends and family to just make them happy!

All Rights Reserved. Colorful Swearing Dreams

No part of this book may be reproduced, stored in a retrieval system, or transmitted in any form or by any means, electronic, mechanical, photocopying, recording, or otherwise, without the prior written permission of the author.

Colorful Swearing Dreams

Swear Word Coloring Book for Adults

Made in United States
Troutdale, OR
11/30/2024